weatheregg™ kids: Weather from A-Z: Coloring Book

Copyright © 2017 by Linda Rawson

First Edition 2017

ISBN-13: 978-1546791621
ISBN-10: 1546791620

Printed in the United States of America.

Copy Editor: DynaGrace Enterprises - DynaGrace.com
Cover Designer: Linda Rawson
Illustrated by:
    Cover - Glag410
    weatheregg™ Kids - Vektor3d
    Illustrations - Awwibimr
Authored by:
    Linda Rawson
    www.LindaRawson.com
    Email: me@lindarawson.com
Published by:
    DynaGrace Enterprises
    187 W 100 S
    Morgan, UT 84050
    Phone: (800) 676-0058
    E-mail: info@dynagrace.com

weatheregg™ kids

WEATHER FROM A-Z

COLORING BOOK

Linda Rawson

To all the kids who want to learn about science, in particular, weather.

weatheregg™ kids

Holley
Humidity

Wesley
Wind

Tommy
Temperature

Peggy
Pressure

Anemometer

[an-uh-mom-i-ter]

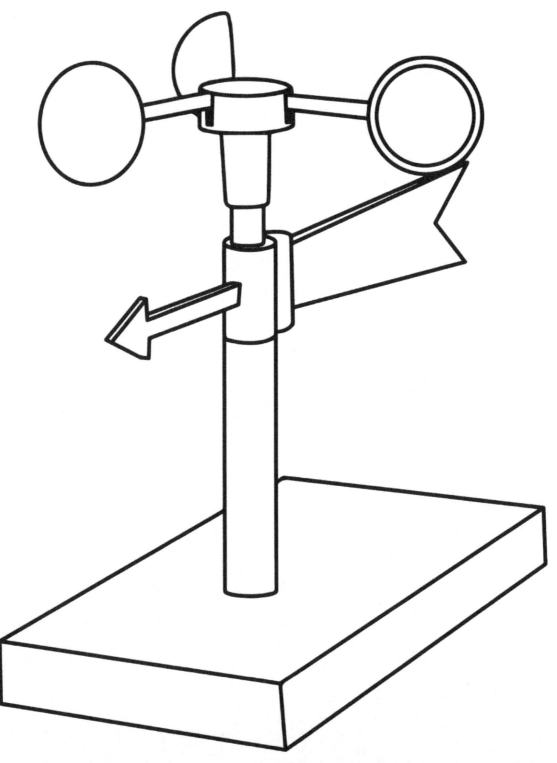

An instrument that measures wind speed in miles or kilometers per hour. The term is derived from the Greek word "*anemos*", which means wind.

Blizzard

[bliz-erd]

Blizzards are winter storms made of blowing snow and wind. Heavy snowfalls and severe cold often accompany blizzards. You cannot see buildings, trees or cars during a blizzard and this situation can be dangerous.

Cumulonimbus

[kyoo-myuh-loh-nim-buh s]

Cumulonimbus clouds are large, tall clouds that are dark on the bottom. They produce rain and thunderstorms. In fact, they are sometimes called thunderstorm clouds, even though they bring other kinds of weather including hail and snow. Seeing a cumulonimbus might get you out of school for a snow day!

weatheregg™ kids: Weather from A-Z

Drought

[drout]

Wherever there is a shortage of rain over a long period of time, there is drought. Drought affects plants, animals, and people by drying up everything. Drought is a problem for farmers and for the people who depend on the crops they produce.

El Niño

[el neen-yoh]

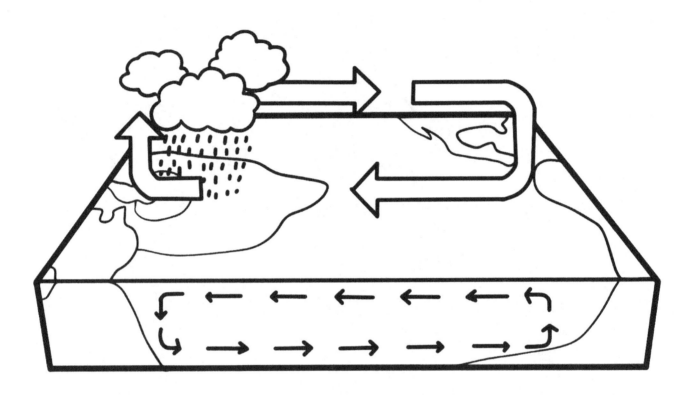

El Niño is a very bad weather condition. The water in the Pacific Ocean by the equator gets hotter than normal and affects the weather around the world. El Niño climate conditions occur every 3 to 7 years, and are not predictable. El Niño causes drought in some areas of the world and flooding in others. El Niño is Spanish for "the boy" and is the opposite of La Niña which means "the girl." La Niña is a cold weather condition that causes snowstorms in some areas and heat waves in others.

Forecast

[fawr-kast]

A prediction of future weather is called a Weather Forecast. A Weather Forecast uses computer models, observations by sensors, and a history of trends and patterns. Forecasts get more accurate as technology gets better.

Ground Fog

[ground fawg]

Ground Fog is condensed water vapor or a cloud floating close to the ground instead of in the sky. Ground Fog prevents you seeing anything like trees or buildings and you see only the Ground Fog.

weatheregg™ kids: Weather from A-Z

Hail

[heyl]

You might know Hail when you see little pieces of snow in your hand shaped like balls. Ice crystals form and begin to fall towards the Earth's surface from within cumulonimbus clouds. As this happens, wind gusts pick up the ice crystals, pushing them back up high into the clouds. As the ice crystals begin to fall again, they continue growing. Like a snowball that rolls down a hill.

Ice Storm

[ahys stawrm]

An ice storm is a type of winter storm caused by freezing rain. Ice storms form when a layer of warm air is between two layers of cold air.

Jet Stream

[jet streem]

A strip of high-speed wind that blows from west to east in the upper atmosphere. This strong wind steers the entire weather system changing the course of the weather.

Knot

[not]

Knots are a unit of wind measurement given on weather charts. It seems strange that a knot is so close to miles per hour. There are 1.15 miles per hour (mph) (1.85 km/h) in 1.00 knots. A 100-knot wind is equal to 115 mpg (185 km/h. The fastest cheetah runs 70 mph (112.65 km/h).

Lightning

[lahyt-ning]

Lightning is an electric charge. Small bits of frozen raindrops bump into each other as they move around in thundercloud. Almost all these collisions create an electric charge. After a while, the whole cloud fills up with electrical charges and produces lightning.

Meteorologist

[mee-tee-uh-rol-uh-jist]

Meteorologists across the world get to predict some of the earth's wildest weather. A meteorologist explains, understands, observes or forecasts the effects weather has on the earth. You should consider being a Meteorologist!

NEXRAD

[neks rad]

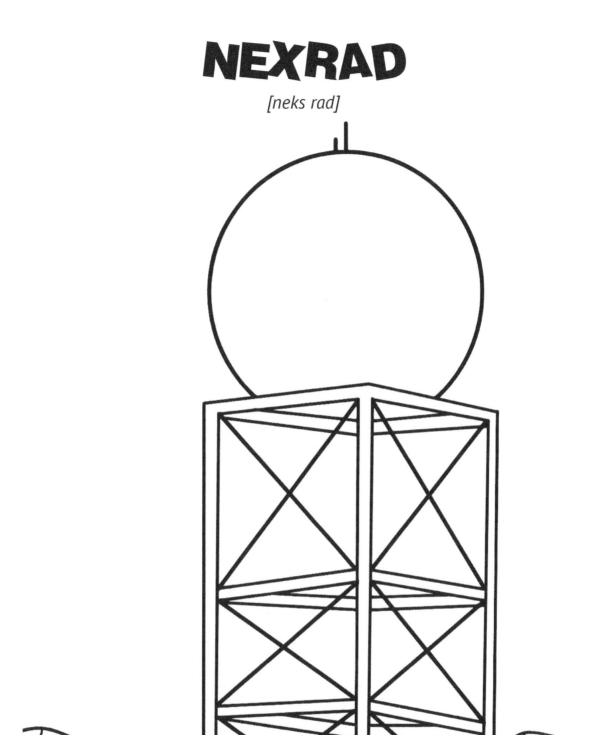

NEXRAD stands for Next-Generation Radar and is a network of 159 Doppler weather radars operated by the National Weather Service. The NEXRAD radar detects precipitation and wind. NEXRAD returns data and displays the data on a map. The maps are very colorful and you see them on Television.

Overcast

[oh-ver-kast]

The sun hides behind gloomy, gray clouds. The sky is covered with gray clouds and the sun peeks through here and there.

Precipitation

[pri-sip-i-tey-shuh n]

The liquid and solid water droplets that fall from clouds and reach the ground are known as precipitation. Precipitation includes drizzle, rain, snow, ice crystals, and hail.

Quasi-stationary Front

[kwey-zahy-stey-shuh-ner-ee fruhnt]

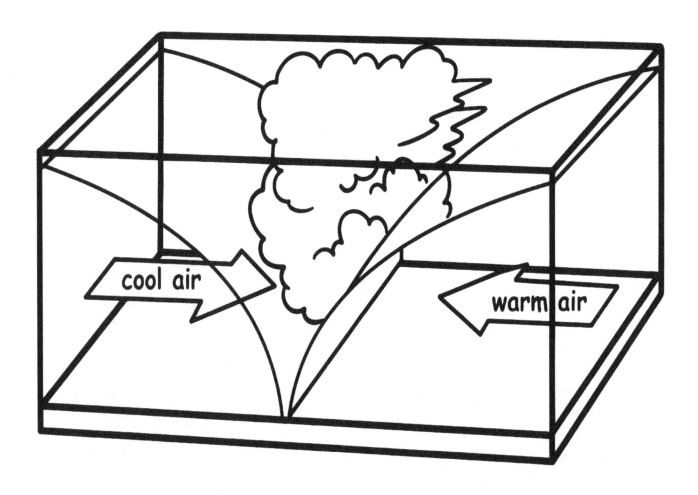

A quasi-stationary front, or stationary front is when two big pieces of air come together but neither displaces the other. A quasi-stationary front can seem like a warm front.

weatheregg™ kids: Weather from A-Z

Rainbow

[reyn-boh]

Rainbows are created by both reflection and bending of light in water droplets in the atmosphere. The result is beautiful, colorful light in the sky with every color shown. No two people see the same rainbow. There is a myth about a pot of gold at the end of the rainbow left by a leprechaun.

Storm

[stawrm]

A storm is a heavy fall of rain, snow, or hail, or a huge outbreak of thunder and lightning, paired with strong winds. Take cover! A storm is coming!

weatheregg™ kids: Weather from A-Z

Tornado

[tawr-ney-doh]

Thunderstorms reach their greatest strength and produce a tornado. A tornado is destructive and has the appearance of a funnel. Tornadoes can destroy buildings, uproot trees and throw vehicles and little children hundreds of yards. Very scary!

Updraft

[uhp-draft]

The upward movement of air in a thunderstorm is known as the updraft, while the downward movement of air is the downdraft. Updrafts are stable. Downdrafts are unstable.

weatheregg™ kids: Weather from A-Z

Vapor
[vey-per]

Water that is in the form of a vapor, or gas is called Vapor. It is a part of the water cycle. Vapor is liquid water heated to boiling temperature, 212° Fahrenheit (100° Celsius). Water Vapor can also be made from ice.

Waterspout

[waw-ter-spout]

A waterspout is just a weak tornado that forms over water. The waterspout is funnel-shaped and are most common along the Gulf Coast. Waterspouts can sometimes move inland, becoming tornadoes causing damage and injuries.

Xerophytes

[zeer-uh-fahyts]

Xerophytes are plants which are adapted to dry/desert areas. To survive these harsh conditions, they have special features. For example, a cactus has white hairs which help to prevent water loss.

Youg

[yoog]

A Youg is a hot wind during unsettled summer weather in the Mediterranean.

weatheregg™ kids: Weather from A-Z

Zonal Flow

[zohn-l floh]

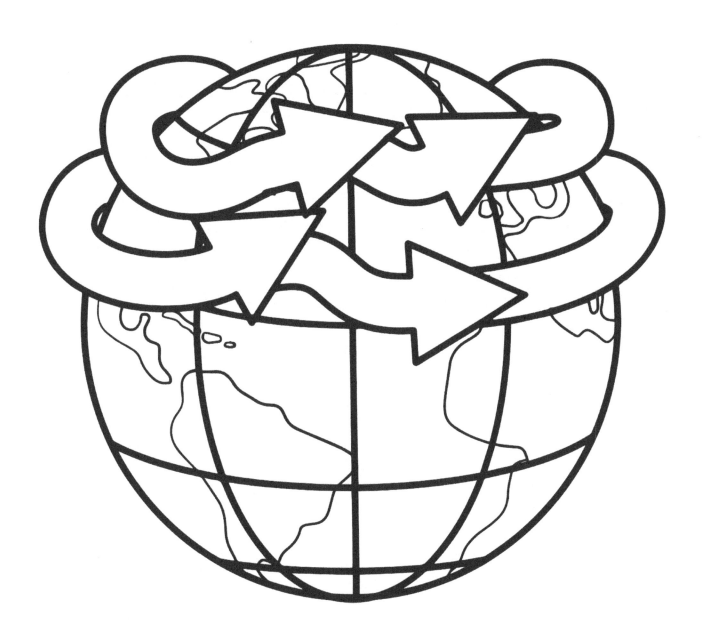

A Zonal Flow is when the winds in the upper levels of the atmosphere blow from coast to coast in a straight line.

Holley Humidity

[hol-ee hyoo-mid-i-tee]

Holley Humidity is full of rain. She loves to rain, and that is why her head is shaped like a raindrop, and she is the color of a raindrop. Humidity is the amount of water vapor in the air. If the humidity is high, your hair will be curly and frizzy and you will feel sweaty and sticky. You will feel much hotter than the temperature says.

weatheregg™ kids: Weather from A-Z

Peggy Pressure

[peg-ee presh-er]

Peggy Pressure is a moody girl. She likes to lower the air pressure which causes storms. When she raises her amulet and calls on Air Pressure, LOOK OUT! Air Pressure is the weight, or heaviness, of air pressing down on earth. We do not get crushed by the massive air pressure because the air pressure inside our body is the same as the atmospheric air pressure. Low pressure often brings bad weather, and high pressure often brings sunny weather.

Tommy Temperature

[tom-ee tem-per-uh-cher]

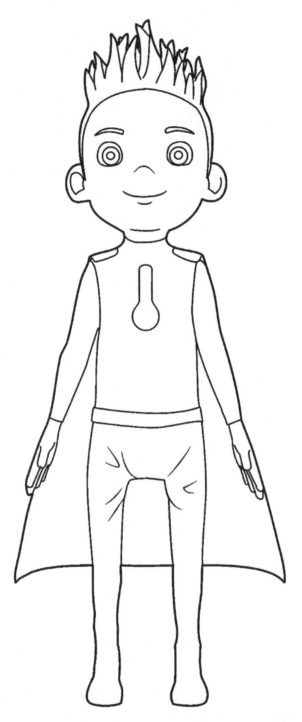

Tommy Temperature raises and lowers temperature. He always tries to do his best, and his cape helps him be a hero. Temperature is a degree of hotness or coldness that can be measured using a thermometer. Temperature is usually measured in either the Fahrenheit or Celsius scale.

Wesley Wind

[wes-lee wahynd]

Wesley Wind can be a mischief-maker. He will blow a nice cool breeze to cool you on a sunny day, or he will be part of a Hurricane. He finds it humorous to change the wind. The wind is air in motion. As the sun warms the earth, the atmosphere warms too. Warm air weighs less than cool air which causes the wind to blow. The wind is measured by wind speed and wind direction.

A-Z Word Search

ANEMOMETER
BLIZZARD
CUMULONIMBUS
DROUGHT
EL NINO
FORECAST
GROUND FOG
HAIL
ICE STORM

JET STREAM
KNOT
LIGHTNING
METEOROLOGIST
NEXRAD
OVERCAST
PRECIPITATION
QUASISTATIONARY

RAINBOW
STORM
TORNADO
UPDRAFT
VAPOR
WATERSPOUT
XEROPHYTES
YOUG
ZONAL FLOW

```
G L B O N I N L E O H N W W O B N I A R
D H S E T Y H P O R E X R V U Q V Q Z D
I X H A A T F A R D P U N V S T U Q A R
S U B M I N O L U M U C F Z L A A H Q U
W L F O R E C A S T Y I P R S T S D T G
S I I D R A Z Z I L B R O I N X K U R M
W G M E S L J V Z Q U O S O T Y O O E Y
O H F H A I L S T S B T I I G P U T D B
L T O R N A D O C C A T C U S N E S J V
F N P K N K C O Z T A E O R D O S W L I
L I H R V R D M I T S Y E F R X R P V D
A N E K J A V O I T K T O O T K E V O G
N G V B R A N P O K A G L A H Z T Q V T
O A X X P A I R C W T O Y U G E E D E V
Z G E O R C M V C Y G Z U H U Y M B R T
U N R Y E M C O Z I D U K P O A O V C P
U J F R R Y P S I J W M S R W M K A K
A F P J E T S T R E A M P A D L E N S F
M J D K L U E P K M R O T S J E N O T M
I M O C A N A T X V T F I G J C A T J S
```

weatheregg™ kids: Weather from A-Z

A-Z Dot to Dot

To receive updates on this book, access to information, videos and downloads that help you with weather visit:

WeatherEgg.com

Key for Word Search

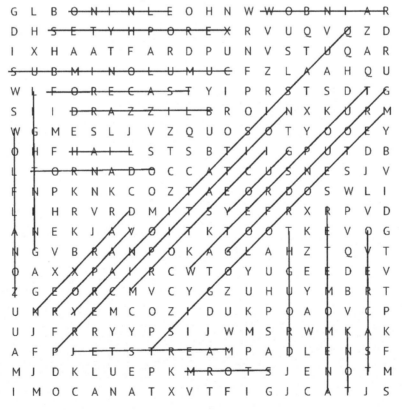

About the Author

Linda Rawson, CEO, and Founder of DynaGrace Enterprises started her company initially called Sensory Technology Consultants, in 2006.

Linda is a technology entrepreneur and executive focused on providing innovative information technology, system integration, cybersecurity and writing services to government and commercial clients. Her background as a software engineer, combined with her corporate executive experience, merges the technical with the business world.

DynaGrace Enterprises is a 100 percent Women-Owned Small Business and is a business run by a family. Jennifer Remund, Linda's daughter, is the Vice President.

Linda was born in a small farming community in Utah. She was raised by her mother, who was a single mom raising five children. Her mother never went to college and did not have any dreams of owning her own business. Because of this, Linda thinks it is important for children, especially girl children, to acquire more knowledge and skills in Science, Technology, Engineering and Mathematics (STEM).

Linda finds pleasure in life by traveling and participating in outdoor activities like golf, hiking, and snowshoeing. She loves meteorology and is an amateur photographer with her companion Scott.

She loves children, especially her grandchildren, nieces and nephews and believes one of the ways to help children learn about science is through something they see every day, which is weather.

Made in the USA
Coppell, TX
31 March 2020